Machine Learning for Beginners

A Comprehensive Beginners Guide to Machine Learning. No Experience Required!

LUKE CARRIER

TABLE OF CONTENTS

Introduction

Congratulations on purchasing *Machine Learning for Beginners* and thank you for doing so.

The following chapters will discuss everything that you need to know to get started with machine learning. There are many different types of computer programming options that you can use, but none of them work as well as machine learning on some complex tasks. When you need to create a spam filter, look through large sets of data, and work on a search engine like feature, machine learning will provide you with the results that you are looking for.

This guidebook will spend some time talking about machine learning and how to get started with the process. We will look at what machine learning is, how it differs from artificial intelligence, some of the basic building blocks of machine learning and how you can add statistics into the mix. We will then end with some information about the three types of machine learning including supervised machine learning, unsupervised machine learning, and reinforced machine learning.

If you are ready to make some unique programs, but you find that traditional forms of programming just aren't going to be able to handle the work, then it is time to bring in machine learning. Take some time to read through this guidebook and learn how to get started with machine learning.

There are plenty of books on this subject on the market, thanks again for choosing this one! Every effort was made to ensure it is full of as much useful information as possible, please enjoy!

Chapter 1

The Basics of Machine Learning

When it comes to the world of information technology, machine learning is really important. You may not have heard about machine learning before, but it's likely that you have used some of its components in your daily life. A good example of this is when you use a search engine like Google or Bing to do a search query. Machine learning helped to make that possible. The program uses machine learning to provide you with the best results, and it can even learn from any choices that you make.

This is just one example of the many technologies that will use machine learning. You can find these not only in search engines but also in spam messages and other applications. Unlike conventional programs you may have learned how to use in the past, machine learning programs are often able to adapt and learn based on the behavior of the user. This makes them more versatile and can ensure that you get the desired results.

A computer that already has machine learning on it can be programmed to learn from the inputs that the user gives it. This will allow the computer to provide the user with the results or answers that are needed, even with complex problems. The input for a learning process, also known as a learning algorithm, will be known here as the data training.

What is machine learning?

With machine learning, you are teaching the computer or the program to use its own experiences with the user in the past to perform better in the future. An example of this would be a program that can help with spam email filtering. There are a few methods that can work in this instance, but the easiest one would be to teach the computer how to categorize, memorize, and then identify all the emails in your inbox that you label as spam when they enter your email. Then, if some new emails come in later that match what is already on your email list, the program would be able to mark these as spam without any work on your part.

While this kind of memorization method is the easiest technique to program and work with, there are still some things that will be lacking with it. First of all, you are missing out on the inductive reasoning in the program, which needs to be there for efficient learning. As a programmer, it is much better to go through and program the computer so that it can learn how to discern the message types that come in and that are spam, rather than trying to get the program to memorize the information.

To keep this process simple, you would program your computer to scan any email that is in the spam folder or already known to be spam. From the scan, your program will recognize some phrases and words that appear and are common in these spam messages. The program could then scan through any new emails that you get, and if an email matches up quite a bit, then it gets automatically sent to the spam folder.

This is a better method to use. But you do need to watch this one a bit. You must pay attention to what is happening during machine learning and realize that sometimes the program may get it wrong. People would be able to look at these emails and use some common sense to figure out if something is spam or not, but the program can't do this. This can result in some normal emails going to your spam folder. The programmer would need to be able to catch the mistakes and work to show the computer program how it can avoid these issues later on in the future.

The benefits of using machine learning

So, at this point, you may be wondering why you would want to learn how to work with machine learning. There are many different things that machine learning can help you with, but there are two main ones that we will focus on right now. The first one includes that using machine learning means that you will be able to handle any task that is too complex for the programmer to place into the computer. The second will include that machine learning can help with adaptively generated tasks that need to be done.

4

With that in mind, let's look at a few situations where you may need machine learning.

Complicated tasks

One way that you can use machine learning is to help with some programming tasks that are complicated. There will be some tasks that you can work on in programming that may not respond that well to conventional programming. These tasks may not have the right amount of clarity that you need to use a conventional program or they just have too much complexity with them.

The first set would be tasks that people and animals can perform. Think about speech recognition, image recognition, and driving as examples of these. Humans can do these just fine, but if you used conventional programming tools to teach the computer how to do this, it will run into trouble. it is much better for the computer to learn the right way to do these tasks by receiving good outputs when they are right. Machine learning can help make this happen.

The second issue is that machine learning can help with tasks that are too hard for humans to do. These would include things such as going through complex analysis where there is too much data for one person to go through well. Companies may decide to use machine learning when they wish to go through a ton of data and make decisions and predictions.

In addition, machine learning can be used in a similar manner to help with genomic data, search engines, and weather prediction. There will be some valuable information in all of the data sets, but humans may not have the energy or the time to go through this information, at least not in a timely manner so they will use machine learning to do it for them.

While traditional forms of programming can do a lot of neat things and have worked for years to help programmers get things done, there are some tasks that just don't work that well with these. Machine learning can fill in the gaps and get you the results that you are looking for.

Adaptively generated tasks

You will find that conventional programs can do a lot of really cool things, but there are some limitations to watch out for. One of these limitations is that these conventional programs are a little bit rigid. Once you write out the code and implement it, the codes will stay the same all the time. These codes will do the same thing over and over unless the programmer changes the code, but it can't learn and adapt.

There will be times when you are working on a program that you want to act in a different manner or react to an input that it receives. Working with a conventional program will not allow this to happen. But working with machine learning allows you to work with a method that teaches the program how to change. Spam detection in your email showed a good example of how this can work.

Easy to work with

While there are some tasks and algorithms that we will talk about later on may seem complicated, they are really neat examples of what you can do with machine learning. These tasks are complicated with a conventional programming, but this is where machine learning will come into play. Things like speech recognition and facial recognition may be hard to do with conventional programming, but with machine learning, you can get it done in no time.

Machine learning is a great program to work with because it can learn as it goes along. Let's take a look at speech recognition. The program may start out having trouble with understanding the user when it first starts. You may find that you need to repeat the word a few times to get the program to work and understand you.

But as you keep using it, the program will start recognizing what you are saying. It will know your accent and the ways that you say some words that may be different than the way others say about it. The program can even get better at making predictions that are right for you and providing answers for the user the longer that the program is used.

The program will be able to do this learning, no matter what kind of device it is on so it can learn the way that each person who uses the program likes to speak. When it comes to a traditional programming language, this can be really hard to accomplish and would need some really complex coding. But when you use machine learning, it is something that you can get done in no time.

While machine learning can do a number of complex actions with it, you will find that it is much easier to work with than you would assume. If you have worked with other programming languages in the past, you will find that it doesn't take that long to learn how to work with machine learning. And since there are a ton of different options, including the supervised, unsupervised, and reinforcement machine learning that we will talk about later in this book, you are sure to be able to find the type that can help you get your project completed in no time.

Now that we have taken a quick look at some of the basics that come with machine learning, it is time to move on to some more in-depth information so that you can start using machine learning for your needs.

Applications of machine learning

As you start looking at machine learning, you may notice that it has changed a lot over the years and the different things that programmers are now able to do with it are pretty unique and fun. There are many established firms, as well as startups, that are using machine learning because it has done some amazing things to help their business grow. While there are a lot of applications that machine learning can help you out with, some of the methods that are the best to use include:

- Statistical research: machine learning is a big part of IT now. You will find that machine learning will help you to go through a lot of complexity when looking through large data patterns. Some of the options that will use statistical research include search engines, credit cards, and filtering spam messages.

- Big data analysis: many companies need to be able to get through a lot of data in a short amount of time. They use this data to recognize how their customers spend money and even to make decisions and predictions about the future. This used to take a long time to have someone sit through and look at the data, but now machine learning can do the process faster and much more efficiently. Options like election campaigns, medical fields, and retail stores have used machine learning for this purpose.

- Finances: some finance companies have also used machine learning. Stock trading online has seen a rise in the use of machine learning to help make efficient and safe decisions and so much more.

As mentioned, these are only a few of the ways that you could use machine learning to help your business. As you add it to your business and add some IT to it, you will find that even more options will become available.

What can machine learning help with?

There are actually a lot of different ways that machine learning can help you out with. This is a great tool that many companies and programmers are exploring because it opens up a world of options when it comes to what you can do, especially when it is compared to what traditional programming languages can do. Some of the different challenges that machine learning can help with include:

- Search engines: A really good example of machine learning is with search engines. A search engine will be able to learn from the results that you push when you do a search. The first few times, it may not be as accurate because there are so many options, and you may end up picking an option that is further down the page. But as you do more searches, the program will learn what your preferences are, and it can get better at presenting you with the choices that you want.

- Collaborative filtering: This is a challenge that a lot of online retailers can run into because they will use it to help them get more profits through sales. Think about when you are on a site like Amazon.com. After you do a few searches, you will then get recommendations for other products that you may want to try out. Amazon.com uses machine learning to figure out what items you would actually be interested in, in the hopes of helping you to make another purchase.

- Automatic translation: If you are working with a program that needs to translate things, then you are working with machine learning. The program needs to be able to look at a document and then recognize and understand the words that are there along with the syntax, grammar, and context of the words that are there. And then if there are mistakes in the original document, this can make it harder for the program to learn along the way. The process of machine learning needs to teach the program how to translate a language from one point to another, and if it can do this with more than two languages, then it needs to learn all the different rules of grammar between each one. The programs that are out right now for this are still in beginner stages, so it's important that machine learning is used to improve them.

- Name identity recognition: This is when the program can identify various entities, such as titles, names, places, and actions, out of a document that it reads. This is something that machine learning can do. This can be used when you are working with a program that should digest and then comprehend a document that you give to it. Let's say that you are looking at an email server like Gmail. Some of these are being sent out to new customers with the ability to see a new email address as soon as it shows up in your inbox. It would then automatically take that information and add it to your address book, helping you to keep that information and save time.

- Speech recognition: Machine learning is now starting to learn how to do speech recognition. This can be hard sometimes because there are different languages, different dialects, and even different genders sound different. The way that you say a word may be different than how someone else says the same word. But with products like the Amazon Echo, machine learning is coming to the forefront as a way to make these products work. They can slowly learn the way that you talk and to start responding appropriately. In the beginning, there will be mistakes, and it may not fully understand what you are saying. But as you use it more, the device will be able to do better thanks to machine learning.

- Facial recognition: Machine learning can help you out with facial recognition as well. This will require the system to work on several layers to figure out if the person in the picture is someone that it knows. This type would rely on photos as well as videos so that only the people who hold the right authorization would be able to use that system. The system would look at these videos and photos and figure out who is allowed on the system. Through a series of learning processes, it would then tell who can get onto the system and who is not allowed there. If this is not set up the right way, then you may end up with those who are authorized not getting in and those without the proper authorization being able to get in. Machine learning will be able to provide you with the tools that you need to get this done.

Machine learning is really great for helping you to figure out some complex technical issues that are pretty much impossible to do accurately with conventional programming. Many of the algorithms that we discussed in the rest of this guidebook will help you to deal with these common issues so that you can get them to work for your program. Whether you want to work on a search engine like program, facial recognition, speech recognition or some other common issue in your programming, machine learning will be able to help you get it done.

Chapter 2

Are Machine Learning and Artificial Intelligence the Same?

Machine learning can work really well when it comes to the field of data science as well as artificial intelligence. To start, data science is a pretty broad term that will include different concepts. One of these concepts is machine learning, but it can also include artificial intelligence, big data, and data mining to name a few. Data science is actually a newer field that is growing as people find more uses for computers and use them more often.

Statistics is really important when it comes to data science, and it can also be used often when it comes to machine learning. You would be able to work with classical statistics, even at the higher levels, so that the data set will stay consistent throughout. But the way that you use it will depend on what kinds of data you are using and how complex the information gets.

It is important to understand the difference between the categories of artificial intelligence and machine learning. There are some instances where they can be very similar, but there are some major differences, which is why they are considered two different things. Let's take a look at each of these to ensure that we understand how they both work in data science.

Artificial intelligence.

The first thing we will take a look at is artificial intelligence – AI. This is a term that was first brought about by a computer scientist named John McCarthy in the 1950s. AI was first described as a method that you would use for manufactured devices to learn how to copy the capabilities of humans in regards to mental tasks.

However, the term has changed a bit in modern times, but you will find that the basic idea is the same. When you implement AI, you are enabling machines, such as computers, to operate and think just like the human brain can. This is a benefit that means that these AI devices are more efficient at completing some tasks than the human brain.

At first glance, this may seem like AI is the same as machine learning, but they are not exactly the same. Some people who don't understand how these two terms work can think that they are the same, but the way that you use them in programming will make a big difference.

Machine learning

Machine learning is a little bit newer than some of the other parts of data science, only about twenty years old. But even though it has been around for that long, it has only been in the past few years that computers have been changed so that they can catch up with machine learning

Machine learning is a section of data science that focuses specifically on having the program learn from the input and the data that the user gives to it. This helps it to make predictions in the future. For example, when you use a search engine, you would put in a term that you want to search into the bar and the engine would go through all the pages that are online to see what is available and will match what you want to know.

The first few times that you do these search queries, it is likely that the results will have something of interest, but you may have to go down the page a bit to find the information that you want. But as you keep doing this, the computer will take that information and learn from it to provide you with choices that are better in the future. The first times, you may click on like the sixth result, but over time, you may click on the first or second result because the computer has learned what you find valuable.

With traditional programming, this is not something that your computer can do on its own. Each person searches differently, and there are millions of pages to sort through. Plus, each person who is doing their searches online will have their own preferences for what they want to show up. Conventional programming will run into issues when you try to do this kind of task because there are just too many variables. Machine learning has the capabilities to make it happen though.

Of course, this is just one example of how you can use machine learning. In fact, machine learning can help you do some of these complex problems that you want the computer to solve. Sometimes you can solve these issues with the human brain, but you will often find that machine learning is more efficient and faster than what the human brain can do.

An example of this is working with data mining. This often includes a ton of data, enough that it is hard for a person to go through it and gather the information in a timely or efficient manner. Machine learning would be able to look through this information and provide the company with some predictions that they should take based on that data.

Of course, a human could go through and look at all of this information, but there is often too much. They may be confused at all the information, have no idea how to sort through it, and it is easy to miss stuff. And with all that information, it could take a person so long to do it that the data is outdated by the time they get done. Machine learning can handle all of that work for you and get results back in a fraction of the time, which is why a lot of businesses find that this is a great program to add into their business model.

Now that you know a little bit more about machine learning and how it does have some differences from artificial intelligence, it is time to add in statistics to the mix and see how this will be a great way to help you get more done with machine learning.

Chapter 3

Using the Probability and Statistics to Help with Machine Learning

You will find that with machine learning, it is important to recognize that there will be a relationship that will form between this process and the probability theory. Machine learning can be a broad field, and this means that it can intersect with some other fields. The fields that it interacts with will depend on the specific project you will work with. Probability and statistics often merge with machine learning so understanding how these three can work together can be important for your project.

There are a few different ways that statistics and the probability theory will be really important to the whole learning process that goes on with machine learning. First, you have to be able to pick out the right algorithm, and there are quite a few different ones that you can pick from as you will see later on as we progress through this book. The algorithm that you end up picking out needs to have a good balance of things like accuracy, training time, complexity, and a number of parameters. And as you work more with machine learning, you will notice that each project will need a different combination of these factors.

Using the probability theory and statistics, you can better pick out the right parameters for the program, the validation strategies, and make sure that you pick out the right algorithm for your needs. They can be helpful as well for letting you know what level of uncertainty is present inside of your choice so you can guess how much you can trust what is going on.

The probability theory and statistics will help you out quite a bit when it comes to working in machine learning and can help you to understand what is going on with the projects you are working on. This chapter will take a look at the concepts that you need to know about these topics so that we can use them later on with machine learning.

Looking at random variables

Now, the first topic we need to look at when it comes to statistics is random variables. With probability theory, these random variables will be expressed with the "X" symbol, and it is the variable that has all its possible variables come out as numerical outcomes that will come up during one of your random experiments. With random variables, there will be either continuous or discrete options. This means that sometimes your random variables will be functions that will map outcomes to the real value inside their space. We will look at a few examples of this one to help it make sense later on.

We will start out with an example of a random variable by throwing a die. The random variable that we will look at will be represented by X, and it will rely on the outcome that you will get once the die is thrown.

The choices of X that would come naturally here will go through to map out the outcome denoted as 1 to the value of i.

What this means is that if X equals 1, you would map the event of throwing a one on your die to being the value of i. You would be able to map this out with any number that is on the die, and it is even possible to take it to the next step and pick out some mappings that are a bit strange. For example, you could map out Y to make it the outcome of 0. This can be a hard process to do, and we aren't going to spend much time on it, but it can help you to see how it works. When we are ready to write out his one, we would have the probability, which is shown as P of outcome 1 of random variable X. it would look like the following:

$$PX(i) \text{ or } (x=i)$$

Distribution

Now we need to look at what the probability distribution is like with this process. What we mean here is that we will look at see what the probability of each outcome will be for the random variable. Or, to make it simple, we will see how likely it is that we will get a specific number, like a six or a three, when we throw the die.

To get started with this, we will need to look at an example. We will let the X, or the random variable, be our outcome that we get once the diet is thrown. We will also start with the assumption that the die is not loaded so that all six sides will have the same probability of showing up each time that you throw the diet. The probability distribution for throwing your die and getting a specific number includes:

$$PX(1) = PX(2) = \ldots = PX(6) = 1/6$$

In this example, it matches up to the what we did with the random variables, it does have a different type of meaning. Your probability distribution is more about the spectrum of events that can happen, while our random variable example is all about which variables are

18

there. With the probability theory, the P(X) part will note that we are working with our probability distribution of the random variable X.

While looking through these examples, you can notice that your distribution will sometimes include two or more variables at the same time. When this happens, we will call it a joint distribution. Your probability will now be determined by each of the variables if there are more than one, that is now involved.

To see how this process will work, let's say that the X is random and that it is defined by what outcome you get when you throw the die, and the Y will be a random variable that will tell you what results that you get when you flip a coin. We will assign a 1 to this coin toss if we get heads at the end, and a 0 will show up if you get tails. This makes it easier when we figure out what the probability distribution is for both of these variables.

We will denote this joint distribution as P(X,Y) and the probability of X as having an outcome of a and Y as having an outcome of b as either P(x =a, Y =b) or PX,Y(a,b).

Conditional distribution

We also need to take some time to talk about conditional distribution. When we have an idea about what the distribution of our random variable is because we already know the value of one other random variable, then we can base the probability of the event on the given outcome of the other event. So, when we are looking at the conditional probability of your random variable called X when X=2, given that the variable Y is Y=b, you can use the following statement to help you define both of these variables:

$$P(X = a | Y = b) = P(X = a, Y = b)/P(Y = b).$$

As you work through machine learning, there will be a few times when you may need to use conditional distributions. These can be good tools depending on the system that you are designing, especially if you need to have the program reason with uncertainty.

Independence

Another variable that you can work with when doing machine learning is to figure out how much independence the problem has. When you are doing random variables, you will find that they will end up being independent of what the other random variables are as long as the variable distribution doesn't change when a new variable is introduced to the equation.

You can make some assumptions about your data in machine learning to help make things easier when you already know about the independence. An example of this is the training sample of "j and i" will be independent of any underlying space when the label of sample "i" is unaffected by the features sample "j". No matter what one of the variables turns out, the other one is not going to be affected by that.

Think back to the example of the die and the coin flip. It doesn't matter what number shows up on the die. The coin will have its own result. And the same can be said the other way around as well. The X random variable is always going to be independent of the Y variable. It doesn't matter the value of Y, but the following code needs to be true for it:

$$P(X) = P(X|Y).$$

In the case above, the values that come up for X and for Y variables are dropped because, at this point, the values of these variables are not going to matter that much. But with the statement above, it is true for any type of value that you provide to your X or Y, so it isn't going to matter what values are placed in this equation.

This chapter went over just a few of the things that you can do with the help of probability theory and statistics when you are working on machine learning. You can experiment with some of these to get the hang of what you can do with their use and then learn a few more algorithms that you can use later on.

Chapter 4

The Building Blocks Needed
for Machine Learning

There are some algorithms that you will want to learn how to use to do well when you work on machine learning. But before we get to those, it is important to learn a few of the basic building blocks of machine learning. Doing this will really help you when you are ready to work with the machine learning algorithms.

These algorithms are great because they help you to do a lot of amazing things in machine learning, and they are the main reason why you would want to use machine learning. This chapter will help you to learn some of the basics of machine learning so that you can get started and be ready to take on some of the more advanced stuff later on.

The learning framework

In the last chapter, we talked about some of the statistics that go behind machine learning. When you use some of the contexts that we talked about before, it is easier to simplify the whole process of learning that the computer goes through. Let's look at an example of this.

Let's say that you decide that it is time to go on vacation to a new island. The natives that you meet on this island are really interested in eating papaya, but you have very limited experience with this kind of food. But you decide that it is good to give it a try and head on down to the marketplace, hoping to figure out which papaya is the best and will taste good to you.

Now, you have a few options as to how you would figure out which papaya is the best for you. You could start by asking some people at the marketplace which papayas are the best. But since everyone will have their own opinion about it, you will end up with lots of answers. You can also use some of your past experiences to do it.

At some point or another, you have worked with fresh fruit. You could use this to help you to make a good choice. You may look at the color of the papaya and the softness to help you make a decision. As you look through the papaya, you will notice that there are a ton of colors, from dark browns to reds, and even different degrees of softness, so it is confusing to know what will work the best.

After you look through the papayas a bit, you will want to come up with a model that you can use that helps you to learn the best papaya for next time. We will call this model a formal statistical learning framework, and there will be four main components to this framework that includes:

- Learner's input

- Learner's output

- A measure of success

- Simple data generalization

Learner's input

The first section of the framework that you need to look at is called the learner's input. To do this, you need to find a domain set and then focus on it. This domain can be an arbitrary set that is found in the objects, which in this framework is known as the points, that you need to get labeled. So, going back to the exercise about the papaya, you would have the domain set be any of the papayas that you are checking out. Then the domain points would be able to use the vectors of features, which in this case includes the softness and color of the fruit.

Once you have determined what domain points and domain sets you want to use, you can then go through and create the label set that you will use. In this exercise, the label set will hold onto the predictions that you will make about the papayas. You can look at each papaya and then make a prediction on how it tastes and whether it is the best one for you.

The label set that you get with this exercise will have two elements. The X will be any of the papayas that you think will taste bad. And then the Y will be the ones that you feel taste the best.

From here, you can work on what is known as the training data. This training data will be a set which can hold the sequence pairs that you will use when testing the accuracy of your predictions. So, with the exercise of the papayas, the training data will be the papayas that you decide to purchase. You will then take these home and taste them to see what tastes the best. This can help you to make better decisions later on when you purchase papayas. If you find that you really like a specific softness or color, ensure that you purchase that kind the next time.

Learner's output

Now that you have your input in, you will want to work on the output. The output is basically going to be the creation of a rule of prediction. It often goes by the name of predictor, classifier, or hypothesis, which you will then use to take the domain points and label them. With the papaya example, this rule will be the standard, which you get to set to where you want, and which will be used to help you figure out whether a papaya that you purchase will taste good or not, even before you eat it in the future.

When you first start, you are basically making guesses because you have no idea which papaya will be good or not. You can use some of your experiences from the past to help if you want, but since you haven't had a papaya before, it is hard to know what will taste good or not. But as you try out papayas and get some more experience with them, you will find that your future predictions will get much better.

Data generalization model

Once you have done the learner's input and output, you will need to take a look at what is known as a data generalization model. This model is nice because it can help you to create your own data for training based on the probability distribution of the domain sets that you used with the papayas. With this example, the model will be the method that you will use to decide what papayas you want to grab at the market to test them out at home.

In the beginning, you may not have any idea of what the distribution is. The data generalization model is designed to help you out, even if you don't know which ones to pick out from the beginning.

Measure of success

Before you can take time to work with the model above, you must make sure that you have some sort of method in place that can help you figure out whether you are successful or not in the project. There are a ton of options that you can choose with the papayas, but there must be some indicator along the way that will help you make the best predictions about whether you will see that success that you want or not.

Since the goal of this experiment is to help you figure out the fruits that will taste the best, so you are set in the future to get the ones that you like, you can use the error of the predictor simply by making sure that you pick out a range of different types of papayas when you are at the market. With all of this variety, it is easier to taste them at home and figure out which ones you like the most. Make sure to write down your observations as you eat each one. This will help you when you go back to the market because then you are more likely to pick out the fruits that you like the best.

PAC learning strategies

While we spent some time talking about how to set up a hypothesis and a training data set to get started with learning strategies in the above section, we still haven't spent time learning about PAC learning, There are two parameters that need to be found in this kind of learning including the accuracy parameter and the output classifier.

First, we need to look at the accuracy parameter. This is the parameter that will be used to determine how often the output classifier that you set up at the start will be able to make correct predictions. These predictions need to be set up to be based on information that you provide. You can also work with what is known as a confidence parameter. This parameter will measure how likely it is that your predictor can reach a certain level of accuracy. Accuracy can be important based on the type of project that you are working on so you should definitely look into this kind of learning if your project needs to maintain a high level of accuracy.

There are several ways that PAC can come in handy when you are doing a project. You may want to use it when you do training data to help see how accurate the model you have is. you may want to bring it into the learning when you feel that some uncertainties will come up and you want to ensure that your computer can handle them. Keep in mind that any time you work with the PAC learning model, it is always going to generate a few random training sets that you should watch out for.

Generalization models in machine learning

In machine learning, when you are considering what the idea of generalization is about, you are basically seeing that there are two components present and you will need to use both of them before you can get through all the data. The components that need to be present include the reliability assumption and revisiting the true error rate.

Any time that you can work with this, and you can meet the reliability assumption, you will be able to expect that the algorithm that you use in machine learning to get the results is pretty reliable for helping you know the distribution. But, there are also times when the assumption that you make here is not going to be very practical. This means that the standards that you picked out may have been unrealistic and that you went with the wrong algorithm to get all the work done.

In addition, the type of algorithm that you try to pick out for machine learning doesn't guarantee that you come up with a hypothesis that is something you like. Unlike using the Bayes predictor, which is an algorithm we will talk about more, later on, these algorithms are not set up to find which type of error rate is the best for you either.

In machine learning, there will be times when you need to make assumptions and use the experience that you have, either in that area or a similar area, to get things done. In some cases, you may even need to do some experimenting to figure out what you want to do. But machine learning can help to get this done.

These are the basic building blocks that you will need to understand and use when you are doing machine learning. These are so important because they can help you see how the programs that run on machine learning are working. You will then be able to use this information in the proceeding chapters to help you when we look through the different machine learning algorithms.

Chapter 5

Supervised Machine Learning

Now that we know a little bit more about machine learning and some of the basic building blocks that come with it, it is time to take a closer look at the different types of machine learning and how they work. To start with, there are three basic types of machine learning that you can use. These will include reinforcement learning, unsupervised learning, and supervised learning. All of these work in slightly different ways, but they will help the computer learn how to react to the input it gets from the user. The one that you will pick out depends on what project type you want to work with.

Let's start with the first machine learning technique that is called supervised machine learning. Supervised learning will occur when you pick out an algorithm that can learn the right response to the data a user inputs to it. There are several ways that supervised machine learning can do this. It can look at examples and other targeted responses that you provide to the computer. You could include values or strings of labels to help the program learn the right way to behave.

This is a simple process to work with, but an example to look at is when a teacher is teaching their students a new topic, and they will show the class examples of the situation. The students would then learn how to memorize these examples because the examples will provide general rules about the topic. Then, when they see these examples, or things that are similar, they know how to respond. However, if an example is shown that isn't similar to what the class was shown, then they know how to respond as well.

When it comes to the learning algorithms that you can use with supervised machine learning, there are a few types that you can pick from. The most common types include:

- Decision trees

- Regression algorithms

- KNN

- Random forest

Decision trees

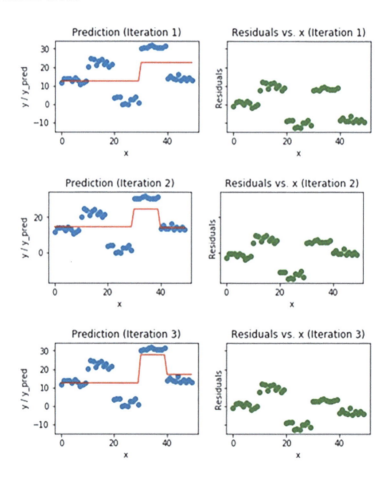

The first type of algorithm that you can use is known as decision trees. These are very efficient data tools if you would like to take a look at several different choices and then pick the right decision out of them for you or for your business. When these different options are presented to you, you will be able to see all the possibilities and the outcomes from each one, which helps you to make more accurate predictions when it comes to making decisions that are the best for your needs.

You can use these decision trees for either continuous random variables or other categorical variables. However, most of the time you will use decision trees to help with problems of classification. To create a good decision tree, you must split up your whole set of domains so that you end up with at least two sets, but often more, of similar data. These are then sorted out with the help of their independent variables because it can help to distinguish between the different sets.

So, how is this all going to work? We will start out with the idea of 60 people in a class. These students will have three independent variables including their heights, their class, or their gender. When you look at these 60 students in the class, you already know before you start that 30 of these students like to spend their free time playing soccer, so you decide to work on a model that can help you figure out which of the students will be the soccer players and which aren't.

To figure this out, the decision tree will be able to look at the students and then divide them up into groups. We would use the variables that we talked about before. The hope is that you would end up with a homogenous set of students when you are done.

There are other algorithms that you will find work well with the decision tree to help you split up the data that you have. This ends up giving you at least two subsets, and they will produce outcomes that are homogenous. Remember that you can have more, but since we are just trying to figure out whether the students are soccer players or not, we just want to split it up into two groups right now.

Decision trees are a great option to work with because they allow you to split up the data and then make some decisions based on that data. It is a great way to ensure that you are making the best decisions for yourself or for your business because you have all the information presented in front of you, rather than just having to guess at the best result.

Random forests

If the decision tree is not the right algorithm for you, you can choose to work with the random forest algorithm. These are popular to use so if you want to learn more about data science, then you would need to learn more about them to help you out. Since random forests are popular and well-known, it is common to see that they will help out with a ton of problems. For example, if you want to work with tasks that explore through your data, like dealing with values that are missing or treating the outliers of your information, then these random forests are a great option to help you get this done.

- Now, there are a few different times when you will want to use random forests because they are perfect for giving you results when other algorithms aren't doing the job. Some of the ways that these random forests can work to your advantage include:

- When you are working on your own training sets, you will find that all of the objects that are inside a set will be generated randomly, and it can be replaced if your random tree things that this is necessary and better for your needs.

- If there are M input variable amounts, then m<M will be specified from the beginning, and it will be held as a constant. The reason that this is so important because it means that each

tree that you have is randomly picked from their own variable using M.

- The goal of each of your random trees will be to find the split that is the best for the variable m.

- As the tree grows, all of these trees will keep getting as big as they possibly can. Remember that these random trees are not going to prune themselves.

- The forest that is created from a random tree can be great because it is much better at predicting certain outcomes. It can do this for you because it will take all prediction from each of the trees that you create and then will be able to select the average for regression or the consensus that you get during classification.

Random forests can be a great tool to use when working on data science and there are many advantages to picking this one instead of one of the other options. First, these random forests can deal with both classification and regression problems, which most other algorithms aren't able to do. In addition, random forests can be great for handling larger amounts of data, and you can add in thousands or more variables, and this algorithm can handle it just fine.

One thing to keep in mind with this one is that while the random trees can work with regression problems, they are not able to make predictions that go past the ranges that you place into the training data. This can help you out with some predictions, but there will be limited since it won't go past the ranges that you can provide so your accuracy will be lower.

KNN algorithm

Another type of algorithm that you can use with supervised machine learning is the KNN, or the k-nearest neighbors, algorithm. When you use this algorithm, you will use it to search throughout all of the data that you have for k most similar examples of whatever data instance you are trying to work on. Once you are successful with this, the KNN algorithm is then able to look through it all and summarize the results before it uses these results to make predictions for that instance.

When you use the KNN algorithm model, you can use this as a way to be competitive in your learning. This works because there is some competition between the different elements in the various models so that it is successful in making predictions.

This one does work a little bit different compared to the other options we have talked about above. It is sometimes seen as a lazier learning process because it is not going to create any models for you until you ask it for a brand new prediction. This is sometimes a good thing depending on the case because it can ensure that the data you are working with is always relevant to the task that you want it for.

There are many benefits that come with using the KNN algorithm. When you pick out this algorithm, you can cut through the noise that is inside your data set. This is because it will rely on a competitive method to sort through the data that you see as desirable. The KNN algorithm is great at handling large amounts of data at the same time, helping you out if you have huge sets of data that need to be gone through.

The biggest issue that comes with using this particular algorithm is that it does have a high computational cost, especially when it compares to the other algorithms. This is because the KNN algorithm will look through all of the data points before it sends out a good prediction for you to look through.

Naïve Bayes

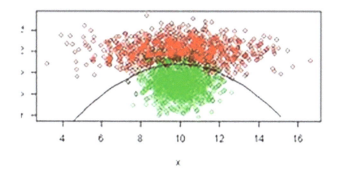

To understand how Naïve Bayes works, we need to use our imaginations a little bit. Imagine that you are working on a scenario that includes classifications problems and you want to create a brand new hypothesis as well as a design some new discussions and features that are based on the importance of each variable. Once you have that kind of information, it is likely that the stakeholders of the company will want to see the model that you are looking to produce, even if it is not done. How are you supposed to present this information if you are not even done with it?

In most cases, you will work with hundreds of thousands of data points that you need to show on the model. There are often other variables that show up in the training set as well. How are you able to show off all this information to your stakeholders as well? And how can you present this in a way that your stakeholders will understand?

The good news is that there is an algorithm that you can work with that will help you to stick with an early stage of the model that is easy to understand while you can still show all of the information that is needed. The algorithm that you will use for this is called the Naïve Bayes algorithm, and it is a great way to use a few demonstrations to showcase your model, even when it is still at an earlier stage of development.

Let's take a look at how this will work with an example of apples. When you grab what is considered an average apple, you will easily be able to state that there are some distinguishing features that are present. This could include the fact that the apple is red, that it is round, and that it will be around three inches round. While these can sometimes be found in some other types of fruits, when all of these features are present together, then we know that the fruit in our hands is an apple. This is a basic way of thinking, but this is an example of working with the Naïve Bayes.

The Naïve Bayes model is meant to be easy for you to put together, and it is sometimes used to help you get through really large sets of data in a way that is simplified. One of the advantages of working with this model is that though it is simple, it is sometimes better to work with compared to the other, more sophisticated models that you can work with.

As you get more familiar with this algorithm, you will find that there are a lot of reasons to use it. The Naïve Bayes' model is easy to use and is effective at predicting the class of your test data sets, so it is the perfect choice for someone who wants to keep things simple or who is new to the whole process. Even though this algorithm is simple, it will perform well, and it has proven that it can do better than some of the other higher-class algorithms in some cases.

You do need to be careful with this one though because there are some negatives to using the Naïve Bayes' algorithm. First, when you are working with categorical variables, and you need to test data that hasn't been through the training dataset, you will find that this model is not able to make a good prediction for you and will assign those data sets a 0 probability. You can add in some other methods that will help to solve this issue, such as the Laplace estimation, but it can be confusing for someone who is brand new to working in machine learning.

This is not going to be the method that you use all of the time, but if you have a lot of information that you are working on, and you need to be able to showcase it in a simplified manner for your shareholders or for anyone else, then working with the Naïve Bayes algorithm is the best option for you.

Regression algorithms

You can also work with an algorithm that is known as a regression analysis. This is a type that will have you investigate what type of relationship that shows up between your predictor variables and your dependent variables. You will often see that this is a great technique to work on when you want to see if there is a causal relationship between the forecasting, the time-series modeling you have, and your variables. The point of working with this algorithm is designed to fit everything onto a line, or a curve, as much as possible, to help you see if there are any common factors that show up.

There are many companies who will use the regression algorithm to help them make great predictions that will increase their profits. You will be able to use it to come up with a great estimation of the sales growth for the company while still basing it on how the economic conditions in the market are doing right at this moment.

The great thing about this is that you can add in any information that you would like to use. You can add in information about the past and the current economy to this particular algorithm, such as your past and current economic information, and then this gives you an idea of how the growth will go in the future. Of course, you do need to have the right information about the company to make this happen.

For example, if you use the regression algorithm and find that your company is growing at the same rate as what other industries are doing in the economy, you would then be able to use this information to help make predictions for how your company will do in the future if the economy does end up changing.

You will find that there are a few variations that come with the regression algorithm and you will need to choose the one that you want based on the information that you are trying to get from the algorithm. Some of the most common regression algorithms that you may want to use with machine learning include:

- Linear regression

- Polynomial regression

- Logistic regression

- Ridge regression

- Stepwise regression

When it comes to working with regression algorithms, you will easily see the relationship that is there between the independent variables and the dependent variables. This algorithm is also there to show what kind of impact will show up if you try to add in or change some of the variables that are in your set of data.

However, there are some shortcomings that come with the regression algorithm. The biggest one is that you will not be able to use this algorithm to help you with some classification problems. The reason that this doesn't work is that it will try too hard to overfit the data in many cases. So any time that you are trying to add in some different constraints to this, the whole process will be really tedious for you to get done.

As you can see, there are a lot of algorithms that you can use when it comes to working on supervised machine learning. Supervised machine learning is a great way to help you make a program that can do the learning on its own, and the type of algorithm that you will use will depend on the project that you want to complete. The different algorithms are all going to have a ton of applications, which are meant to be there to help you look through all the data that you have (no matter how much you have), make predictions, and do some of the other tasks that you may need to complete when you are using them to help with machine learning.

Chapter 6

Unsupervised Machine Learning

As we mentioned a little bit before, there is more than one type of machine learning that you can work with. Supervised learning is the first one. It is designed for you to show examples to the computer and then you teach it how to respond based on the examples that you showed. There are a lot of programs where this kind of technique will work well, but the idea of showing thousands of examples to your computer can seem tedious. Plus, there are many programs where this is not going t work all that well.

This is where unsupervised machine learning can come into play. We are now going to explore more of what this unsupervised machine learning is all about. Unsupervised learning is the type that will happen when your algorithm can learn either from mistakes or examples without having an associated response that goes with it. What this means is that with these algorithms, they will be in charge of figuring out and analyzing the data patterns based on the input that you give it.

Now, there will also be a few different types of algorithms that can work well with unsupervised machine learning. Whichever algorithm you choose to go with, it can take that data and restructure it so that all the data will fall into classes. This makes it much easier for you to look over that information later. Unsupervised machine learning is often the one that you will use because it can set up the computer to do most of the work without requiring a human being there and writing out all the instructions for the computer.

A good example of this is if your company wants to read through a ton of data to make predictions about that information. It can also be used in most search engines to give accurate results.

There are a lot of different techniques that you can use when it comes to machine learning. Some of the most common methods include:

- Markov algorithm

- Clustering algorithm

- Neural networks

Clustering algorithms

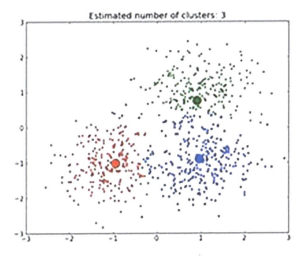

Estimated number of clusters: 3

The first type of machine learning that we will look at is called the clustering algorithm. With the clustering algorithm, we will keep it pretty simple. This method can take our data and then classify it into clusters. Before the program even starts, you get the benefit of picking out how many clusters you would like all the information to fit into. For example, you may decide that you want to combine the data into five different clusters. The program would then go through and divide up all the information that you have into five different clusters so that you could look through it.

The nice thing about this algorithm is that it is responsible for doing most of the work for you. This is because it is in charge of how many of your data points will fit into those clusters that you chose. To keep things organized, we will call all of the main clusters that you picked cluster centroids.

So, when you are looking at one of your clusters, and you notice that there are a lot of points inside of it, you can safely make the assumption that all those particular data points have something in common or they are similar. There is some attribute or another that all the data points in one cluster have in common with each other.

Once these original clusters are formed, you can take each of the individual ones and divide them up to get more cluster sets if you would like. You can do this several times, creating more divisions as you go through the steps. In fact, you could potentially go through this enough times that the centroids will stop changing. This is when you know you are done with the process.

There are several reasons why you would want to work with a clustering algorithm to help you get a program started when doing machine learning. First, doing your computations with the help of a clustering algorithm can be easy and cost efficient, especially compared to some of the supervised learning options that we talked about before. If you would like to do a classification problem, the clustering algorithms are efficient at getting it done.

With that said, you do need to use some caution here though. This algorithm is not going to be able to do the work of showing predictions for you. If you end up with centroids that are not categorized the right way, then you may end up with a project that is done the wrong way.

Markov algorithm

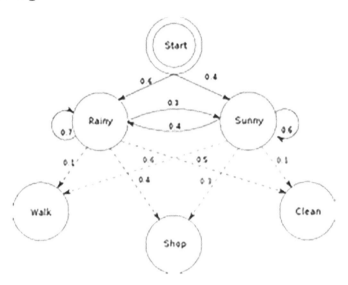

One of the other types of algorithms that you can use with unsupervised learning is the Markov algorithm. This algorithm will take all of the data that you input into the system and then translate it to help it work in another coding language. You can set up all the rules ahead of time for how you want this to work. You may find this useful because it will take a string of data and make it more useful when you learn the parameters of how your data will behave.

You will find that there are numerous ways that you can work with this Markov algorithm. One option is when you are working on something like DNA. You would be able to take a sequence of DNA, and then the Markov algorithm can translate these out into numerical values. When you are working with computers, you will find that reading out some numerical values can be a lot easier than trying to read through the strand of DNA.

A good reason why you would need to use the Markov algorithm is that it is great at learning problems when you already know the input you want to use, but you are not sure about the parameters. This algorithm will be able to find insights that are inside of the information. In some cases, these insights are hidden, and this makes it hard for the other algorithms we have discussed to find them.

There are still some downfalls to working with the Markov algorithm. This one can sometimes be difficult to work with because you do need to manually go through and create a new rule any time that you want to bring in a new programming language. If you only want to work with one type of programming language on your project, then this is not going to be a big deal. But many times your program will need to work with several different languages, and going in and making the new rules a bunch of times can get tedious.

Neural networks

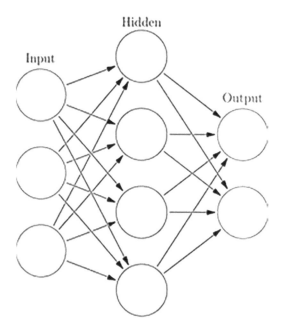

You can also work with neural networks when it comes to unsupervised machine learning. These types of networks will be used a lot because they are great at learning and analyzing patterns by looking at it in several different layers. Each layer that it goes through will spend its time seeing if there is a pattern that is inside the image. If the neural network does find a new pattern, it will activate the process to help the next layer start. This process will continue going on and on until all the layers in that algorithm are created, and the program can predict what is in the image.

Now, there will be several things that will happen from this point. If the algorithm went through all the layers and then was able to use that information to make an accurate prediction, the neurons will become stronger. This results in a good association between the patterns and the object and the system will be more efficient at doing this the next time you use the program.

This may seem a bit complicated so let's take a look at how these neural networks will work together. Let's say that you are trying to create a program that can take the input of a picture and then recognize that there is a car in that picture. It will be able to do this based on the features that are in the car, including the color of the car, the number on the license plate, and even more.

When you are working with some of the conventional coding methods that are available, this process can be really difficult to do. You will find that the neural network system can make this a really easy system to work with.

For the algorithm to work, you would need to provide the system with an image of the car. The neural network would then be able to look over the picture. It would start with the first layer, which would be the outside edges of the car. Then it would go through a number of other layers that help the neural network understand if there were any unique characteristics that are present in the picture that outlines that it is a car. If the program is good at doing the job, it will get better at finding some of the smallest details of the car, including things like its windows and even wheel patterns.

There could potentially be a lot of different layers that come with this one, but the more layers and details that the neural network can find, the more accurately it will be able to predict what kind of car is in front of it. If your neural network is accurate in identifying the car model, it will learn from this lesson. It will remember some of these patterns and characteristics that showed up in the car model and will store them for use later. The next time that they encounter the same kind of car model, they will be able to make a prediction pretty quickly.

This particular algorithm is one that will often be used when you are trying to go through pictures and sort out defining features. It could be used as a face recognition software where you wouldn't be able to put in all of the information ahead of time. It works for defining car models, recognizing different animals, and more.

One of the advantages that you will enjoy when you use neural networks is that you won't have to worry about all of the statistical training for this kind of algorithm. Even without the statistics, you will be able to use it to find some of the complex relationships that show up between the dependent and the independent variables, even if these are nonlinear. The biggest issue with using the neural networks is that they will have a pretty high computational cost so it is not always feasible to use them as much as you would like.

Support vector machines

The next thing that you can work with here is known as SVM, or support vector machine. The SVM will be used for many challenges in regression and classification that you come across. With this one, much of the work that you do on problems with classification can make the work tricky, but this kind of algorithm can handle it all no matter what.

When working with SVM, you will be able to take each of the items that are in your data set and then plot them as one point on your n-dimensional space. N will be the number of features that we are using. Then the value of all features will translate to the value found on the coordinates. Your job here is to determine the hyperplane since this is the part that can tell you the difference between the two classes.

There will also be a few support vectors with the SVM algorithm as well, but you will also notice that these will simply end up being the coordinates of the individual observations that you have. Then you can use SVM to be the frontier that helps to separate out all the classes, and there will end up with two of them when you are done that are the line and the hyperplane.

At this point, you may be wondering what it all means and why you would want to work with an SVM. The first thing to look at is the hyperplane. There are often going to be several hyperplanes that you will need to pick from, and of course, you want to make sure that you are getting the one that works the best for your needs. This is the big challenge that comes up, but luckily the process you use will be easy. The steps that are best for helping you to work with the right hyperplane includes:

- We will start out with three hyperplanes that we will call 1, 2, and 3. Then we will spend time figuring out which hyperplane is right so that we can classify the star and the circle.

- The good news is there is a pretty simple rule that you can follow so that it becomes easier to identify which hyperplane is the right one. The hyperplane that you want to go with will be the one that segregates your classes the best.

- That one was easy to work with, but in the next one, our hyperplanes of 1, 2, and 3 are all going through the classes, and they segregate them in a manner that is similar. For example, all of the lines or these hyperplanes will run parallel with each other. From here you may find that it is hard to pick which hyperplane is the right one.

- For the issue that is above, we will need to use what is known as the margin. This is basically the distance that occurs between the hyperplane and the nearest data point from either of the two classes. Then you will be able to get some numbers that can help you out. These numbers may be closer together, but they will point out which hyperplane will be the best.

45

You will find that the example above is not the only time that you will be able to work with SVM to help with this type of machine learning. When you are taking a look at the data points that you have, and you see that there is a clear margin of separation, then the SVM method is most likely the best one to use to help you out. In addition, the effectiveness that you get out of this model will increase any time that you have a project with dimensional spaces that are pretty high. Working on this particular technique can help you to use a subset of training points that come with a decision function, or the support vector, and when the memory of the program you are working on is high enough to allow you to do this.

While there are benefits that you will get with this method depending on the project that you are working on, there are still going to be times when the SVM method is not the best for you. When you work with a data set that is large, the SVM may not provide you with options that are the most accurate. The training time with these larger sets of data can be high, and this will disappoint you if you need to get through the information quickly. And if there are some target classes that are overlapping, the SVM will behave in a way that is different than what you want.

Chapter 7

Reinforcement Machine Learning

Now that we have taken some time to look at supervised and unsupervised machine learning, it is time to work with the third form of machine learning for your projects. This one is known as reinforcement learning, and it will allow you to do a few more things with your projects that the other two options may not allow.

There are some people who see reinforcement learning as the same thing as unsupervised learning because they are so similar, but it is important to understand that they are different. First, the input that is given to these algorithms will need to have some mechanisms for feedback. You can set these up to be either negative or positive based on the algorithm that you decide to write out.

So, whenever you decide to work with reinforcement machine learning, you are working with an option that is like trial and error. Think about when you are working with a younger child. When they do some action that you don't approve of, you will start by telling them to stop, or you may put them in time out or do some other action to let them know that what they did is not fine. But, if that same child does something that you see as good, you will praise them and give them a ton of positive reinforcement. Through these steps, the child is learning what is acceptable behavior and what isn't.

To keep it simple, this is what reinforcement machine learning will be like. It works on the idea of trial and error, and it requires that the application uses an algorithm that helps it to make decisions. It is a good one to go with any time that you are working with an algorithm that should make these decisions without any mistakes and with a good outcome. Of course, it will take some time for your program to learn what it should do. But you can add this into the specific code that you are writing so that your computer program leans how you want it to behave.

Q-learning

There are different types of reinforcement learning that you can work with, and the first option is known as Q-learning. This algorithm will work well if you want to work with temporal difference learning. As you are working with the different types of machine learning, you will probably notice that this one is almost like an off-policy algorithm that can learn an action value function, allowing you to get what you are expecting no matter what state you are in.

Since you can use this particular algorithm for any function that you want, you must go through and list out the specifications for how the user or the learner will select the course of action.

After you, the programmer, go through and then find the action value function that you want to use, then it is time to work on the optimal policy. You can work on constructing this by using the actions that will have the highest value no matter what state you are working with.

A big advantage of working with Q-learning is that you won't need to provide it with models of the environment for you to compare the utility of all your actions. What this means is that you can compare a few or many actions together, and you will not need to worry about the type of environment that you will use with it.

SARSA

The second type of reinforcement machine learning algorithm that you can use if you choose is known as SARSA. This stands for state action reward state action algorithm. For this option, you will take the time to describe the decision process policy that will occur in your Markov algorithm (remember that we talked about this earlier on).

This would then be the main function that you would use with the updated -value which will then rely on whatever the current state of the learner is. It can also include the reward that the learner will get for the selection they make, the action that the learner choose, and then the new state that the learner will be in when they are done with that action. As you can see, there are a ton of different parts that will end up coming together to make the SARSA work for your needs.

While there are many parts that must come together for this one, this is sometimes seen as the safest algorithm for a programmer to use when they are trying to find the solution they want to use. However, there can possibly be times when your learner will end up with a reward that is higher than what the average is for their trials. This is a bigger issue with the SARSA compared to some of the other algorithms that you have.

There are also going to be times when the learner ends up not going with the optimal path either. Depending on how the program decides to react to this, it could bring up some issues with how they learn and how the program will behave for them.

There are times when the reinforcement learning that you do will look pretty similar to what you can find with unsupervised machine learning. However, this option will spend time working on trial and error to see how it solves problems instead. This can actually end up opening up a lot of opportunities that you may not be able to do when you work with supervised or unsupervised machine learning algorithms that we talked about earlier in this guidebook.

Conclusion

Thank for making it through to the end of *Machine Learning for Beginners*, let's hope it was informative and able to provide you with all of the tools you need to achieve your goals whatever they may be.

The next step is to start trying out a few of the things that we have discussed in this guidebook. Machine learning can really take your project to the next level. While conventional programming techniques can do some wonders when it comes to how much you can do with your programs, there are times when it just won't work for your needs. Machine learning can step in and provide you with the results that you need. And this guidebook will go over the different steps that you need to get started with machine learning, whether you want to work with supervised, unsupervised, or reinforcement machine learning on your next project.

When you are ready to learn a little bit more about machine learning and how to get started, make sure to check out this guidebook to help you out!

Finally, if you found this book useful in any way, a review on Amazon is always appreciated!